PROTOCALL 934

HAZARDOUS MATERIALS TECHNICIAN

PROTOCALL 934

HAZARDOUS MATERIALS TECHNICIAN

Ten Fingers and Ten Toes

Workbook/Exam

Kevin L. Miller, CHMM

authorHOUSE®

AuthorHouse™
1663 Liberty Drive
Bloomington, IN 47403
www.authorhouse.com
Phone: 1-800-839-8640

Published by AuthorHouse 12/19/2014

ISBN: 978-1-4969-5872-3 (sc)
ISBN: 978-1-4969-5871-6 (e)

ACKNOWLEDGEMENT

I would like to take this time to recognize all of the people that devote their lives to emergency response, the people which perform their duties daily without hesitation, because they have a passion for helping others.

I would also like to thank my childhood friends Mark, Anthony, and Renee who spent plenty of time with me chasing the fire trucks and chasing the dreams.

And let's not forget a special thanks to my cousin Darryl who is closer than a brother to me, one whom may have always thought he was following, but instead he was just pushing.

PREFACE

This workbook/exam is not designed to replace the HAZARDOUS MATERIALS TECHNICIAN training manual, but it is designed to provide a comprehensive overview of the manual, along with a series of questions *designed to make the student/the reader think.*

This workbook will recapture the important areas and subject matters that were covered during the training.

Along with providing additional information or answer to the questions that may not have been directly covered in the student training manual.

It is recommended that you study and/or take the hazardous materials technician training course before attempting to complete this workbook/exam.

TABLE OF CONTENTS

1. INTRODUCTION

The threat from hazardous material is real and if you are an emergency responder, work at a treatment storage and/or disposal facility, along with working on remediation sites, you must be trained in accordance to the hazardous waste operations and emergency response requirements.

If you wish to be successful as an emergency responder you must have a team and the team members must know their entire role and take that role seriously.

1. Which federal regulation establishes the training requirements for the hazardous materials technician (the emergency responder)?

2. Briefly described the difference between the private industry and the public sector when it comes to chemical spill response?

3. When it comes to emergency response what are the five (5) levels of training?

4. Which regulation focuses on the safe transportation of hazardous materials?

5. What is the definition of a confined space?

6. What is the biggest difference between emergency response and remediation?

7. Briefly describe what is meant by level a protection?

8. What is NIOSH guidebook used for?

9. How would you use the NAERG to respond to a leaking bulk package transporting a class 8 material?

2. TRAINING AND EDUCATION

The training and education section is designed to get the students to understand the importance of receiving quality education and quality training, along with the importance of building a strong foundation based on hazardous materials, chemistry and toxicology.

The student will also understand that when it comes to developing of an emergency response team. That the diversity and flexibility in the team's training along with the team's background can also be extremely important.

1. Give me an example of some of the additional safety training a hazardous material technician may wish to receive?

2. What is the one thing that the hazardous materials technician must always perform during an emergency response incident?

3. T or F persons that are trained at the awareness level may perform action in the exclusion (hot) zone?

4. What are some of the advance training topics or subject matters a supervisor should receive?

5. T or F, you should receive your initial training after you have responded to your first spill.

6. What is the "one" word used by OSHA to describe the instructor's or the person's providing the training?

7. What are some of the requirements for the (29cfr. 1910.1200) hazard communication standard?

8. What are the different levels of training for the emergency responder in accordance with the hazardous waste operations and emergency response requirements?

9. What are some of the exceptions when it comes to safety training?

10. How many additional hours should the supervisor receive for hazardous waste management and in site safety engineering?

3. REGULATIONS AND STANDARDS

This section is designed to give the student/the reader the ability to understand the differences between the regulations and the standards, along with how these regulations and standard may be applicable to the work.

The student will be able to determine which regulations/requirements are enforceable by law and which of these requirements are based on industries best safety practices. These industry practices are commonly be refer to as standards.

There are three (3) primary Codes of Federal Regulations (CFR's) the hazardous material technician must be familiar with.

The first (CFR) is designed for the protection of the environment, the second regulation focuses on the safe transportation of hazardous materials and the third regulation is designed to focus on the safety of the worker.

1) T or F, Standards are based on the best industry safety practices.

2) Which Code of Federal Regulation (CFR) focuses on safety?

3) Which standard gives the worker "The Right to Know" the hazards of the chemicals in the workplace?

4) Which standards uses a color coded diamond shape symbol to identify the hazards of the chemicals stored at a fixed facility?

5) T or F, it is important to determine how the different regulations or standards may apply to you in the work.

6) T or F, Regulations are enforceable by the law.

7) Which regulations must you comply with, while working on a site that last contained hazardous waste drums?

8) Who is responsible for making sure that the site stays in compliance with the rules and regulations?

4. HAZARDOUS WASTE OPERATION AND EMERGENCY RESPONSE

The HAZWOPER regulation maybe easy to explain but it may take a little more time to fully understand or to comprehend the requirements

The student/the reader will understand if you work on a remediation site, at a treatment, storage or disposal facility and/or as an emergency responder you must be trained.

The levels of training needed by the site personnel are based on a person's duties and responsibility, but everyone should receive the initial training.

The categories of training are divided into different levels; these levels of training may range from the basic awareness level to the advance incident commanders level.

Based on your duties and/or your responsibilities you may be required to receive several additional hours of training, along with annual refresher training.

HAZWOPER focuses on the development of the health and safety plans, the site characterization, and the analysis of the threat, site controls, engineering controls, good work practices, and the selection of personal protection equipment, medical monitoring and more.

This regulation also focuses on the importance of establishing a decontamination plan, sanitation control procedures and a hazardous waste management program immediately

1) T or F, if you work at a treatment, storage and/or disposal facility you are not required certification or training.

2) What are the different levels of training in accordance to the hazardous waste operations and emergency response requirements?

3) In order to be certified at the hazardous materials technician level. How many hours of training are required initially? And how many hours of training are required annually.

4) What is meant by engineering controls?

5) What is the primary function of the hazardous material specialist?

6) Why is it important to establish the hot, warm and cold zones?

7) When should you start developing your decontamination plan?

8) What is the difference between site monitoring and personnel monitoring?

9) As a level two (2) technicians trained at the operations level. What are some of the duties that you are too perform?

5. HAZARADOUS MATERIALS TRANSPORTATION

This section is designed to give the student the working knowledge needed in order to successfully identify hazardous materials, hazardous substances and marine pollutants.

The student will have ability to identify the U.S.D.O.T. hazard classifications and have the ability to identify the different markings, the different labels and the different placards needed for transportation.

The student will be able to determine the types of packages needed in order to containerize, to store and to transport hazardous materials.

Once you have containerized the hazardous materials and you have determined that the hazardous material has to be transported.

You must then determine the proper shipping name and then proper shipping description.

The shipper and/or the potential responsible party (PRP) is responsible for the hazardous materials preparation, the labeling, the placarding, the markings and the completion of the shipping documents.

1) How many D.O.T. hazardous material classifications are there?

2) What are the D.O.T. hazardous material classifications?

3) Where can you find the proper shipping description for a hazardous material?

4) What is the definition of a hazardous substance?

5) What is meant by the 1,000 pound rule

6) What is the difference between a bulk and a non-bulk package?

7) T or F, the shipper is responsible for the preparation of all of the shipping papers?

8) Which D.O.T. hazard classification is identified by a Blue placard or label?

9) What is meant by the letters N.O.S. "Not Otherwise Specified"?

10) Briefly describe how you would use the North American Emergency Response Guidebook (NAERG) to respond to a leaking bulk package of a hazardous material that has a white label with a blacked out skull and crossbones?

11) What is a marine pollutant?

12) What is meant by the primary and secondary hazards?

13) Why is the precedence table important?

14) When should you placard table (1) one commodities?

15) What is the orange panel used for in the transportation of hazardous materials?

6. HAZARDOUS WASTE MANAGEMENT

This section is designed to educate the students on the importance of establishing an effective waste management program immediately.

This section will give the student the working knowledge needed to identify the difference between a hazardous waste, a non-hazardous waste and a non-regulated waste material.

And with this knowledge the student will be able to establish a working and an effective waste management program.

The generator and/or the potential responsible party(PRP) is responsible for the management of the hazardous waste.

It is also important that the (student) reader understand, that based on the quantity of hazardous waste generation that the generator may fall under different regulations/requirements.

All hazardous waste are given hazardous waste codes. Waste codes are designed to show the waste characteristics and/or the source of generation.

A hazardous waste can come from a number of different sources and can either be characteristic and/or listed.

The source of generation can help the generator to establish these waste codes, a waste containerization program, a waste segregation program and/or the waste storage accumulation area.

1) What is the definition of a hazardous waste?

2) T or F, a hazardous waste management program will consist of a waste accumulation area, a waste segregation area, waste containerization and a waste tracking system.

3) T or F, the cross contamination of the waste streams can cost the generator or the potential responsible party thousands of dollars in disposal cost?

4) T or F, the generator or the potential responsible party is not responsible for the waste once it has been transported off the site.

5) What is a characteristic waste?

6) T or F, a listed waste is divided into the following divisions; a specific source, a non-specific source, a raw material and/or an acutely toxic raw material.

7) When does the start accumulation date start on the hazardous waste container for a large quantity generator?

8) What is meant by the generator's status?

9) T or F, the hazardous waste transporters are not required to have E.P.A. Identification numbers.

10) What is the name of the shipping document used to transport hazardous waste?

7. FUNDAMENTAL CHEMISTRY

The student/the reader should realize that in order to be successful as a hazardous materials technician you must have a foundation based on ***chemistry***.

Chemistry is the study of matter and matter is anything that occupies space.

Matter can be described in terms of properties, the physical property and/or the chemical properties.

Hazardous materials can be chemical or biological, they can be a metal or a non-metal, they can be organic or inorganic, they can be a mixture, a solution or even compounds.

The student must understand that in some cases the environment may have some effect on the hazardous material. The student should also understand that some materials may also react with moisture, while others maybe air reactive?

Heat can cause some chemicals to become reactive; while in other cases the cold may cause some chemicals to become less reactive (dormant).

The student should be aware that based on the temperature, the hazardous materials may to go through a phase change and this phase change will occasionally give off gases and these gases maybe heavier or lighter than air.

1)   What is the definition of chemistry?

2) T or F, there are two types of properties.

3) What are the three (3) states of matter?

4) T or F, the physical property will include the color, the odor, the taste, and the density, the solubility in water, along with the melting and the freezing point of the material.

5) T or F, a hazardous materials cannot be a metal.

6) From the point of view of an emergency responder, what is the boiling point?

7) T or F, a mixture is a combination of different solutions.

8) When it comes to successfully starting a fire, what is the fire triangle?

9) T or F, the best way to protect you from radioactive materials is through time, distance, and shielding.

10) What is the difference between Kinetic energy and Potential energy?

11) Why is the specific gravity and vapor pressure important?

Bonus question:

Briefly describe "Newton's" first two laws of motion and how these laws of motion may affect you as an emergency responder?

8. BASIC TOXICOLOGY

This section is designed to educate the students on how to protect themselves from the hazards of a chemical or a biological exposure.

The student will become familiar with the routes of entry to the body.

This section also stresses the benefits of handling hazardous materials safely, during emergency response or remediation and/or the treatment, the storage and/ or disposal of hazardous waste material.

The student will be able to see how based on the hazards of the material, how these hazards can directly affect the response or the remediation activity.

The student will also recognized that NIOSH and OSHA has established exposure limits that are designed to inform you of the concentrations and the limits for these hazardous materials you are allowed to be exposed too.

1)   What are the four (4) routes of entry to the body?

2)   T or F, a material that is an inhalation hazard cannot be absorbed into the bloodstream.

3)   T or F, chemicals may pose different hazards based on the temperature.

4) T or F, the purpose of an assessment is to identify the hazards and to identify how these hazards maybe harmful to the body.

5) What is meant by the lethal dose or the lethal concentration of hazardous materials?

6) T or F, some hazardous materials can target specific organs.

7) What are two (2) ways a hazardous materials can affect the worker (the body)?

8) What is meant by an **IDLH** atmosphere?

9) T or F, a hazardous material that is a carcinogen can be dangerous to the genes.

10) T or F, PEL's stands for the Permissible Exposure Limit which was established by the Occupational Safety and Health administration.

9. PERSONAL PROTECTION EQIUPMENT

This section is designed to give the students the working knowledge needed in order to select the personal protection equipment needed during an emergency response event. The selection of the PPE must be made on site. The selection of PPE is based on the hazards and the duties of the team.

The student will understand that there are different levels of protection. These levels of protection are designed to protect the worker from the various hazards associated with the emergency response and the remediation efforts

The student will become familiar with the donning and the duffing of the PPE, the staging, the disposal, the inspections and even the storage of the personal protective equipment.

The student will understand the importance for hearing protection, eye protection, hand/foot protection, skin protection and respiratory protection.

This is the one area I cannot express the importance of an accurate assessment and based on that assessment you will select the **PPE** that is needed.

Anytime PPE is used it must be compatible with the chemical, the biological and the environmental hazards and you should ***never compromise your safety for your comfort.***

1) T or F, one level of personal protection equipment is designed to fit all of the site hazards.

2) T or F, your PPE should be inspected, stored, staged, compatible with the hazardous material, always updated and ready for usage.

3) T or F, respiratory protection training is only required when you are wearing level B protection.

4) Which level of protection is designed to provide the maximum level of skin protection?

5) Why is permeation and absorption important when selecting PPE?

6) T or F, your PPE should always fit and be comfortable, explain?

7) When should you select your PPE?

8) T or F, each chemical/biological agent will pose its own unique hazards.

9) Describe the maximum level of protection and explain when this level of protection should be used.

10) T or F, personal protection equipment (PPE) and chemical protective clothing (CPC) is designed to do are the same thing. Explain?

10. RESPIRATORY PROTECTION

This section is designed to inform the student/the reader on how important it is to protect the respiratory system.

The student will understand the importance of the medical questionnaire, the fit test, having a written respiratory protection program and the importance of the selection of the appropriate respiratory protection.

The student will understand when it is safe to wear an air purifying respirator (APR) and when it is mandatory that you wear a self-contained breathing apparatus (SCBA).

The student will learn how to identify, how to inspect, how to store, how to maintain and even how to properly wear the respiratory protection.

Because the respiratory system is a direct route of entry to the body, we must have a program in place and this program should be taken seriously.

The wearer of the respirator must receive training in order to understand how the respirator **fits** the different **symbols, codes and the coding** system.

1) T or F, when selecting PPE respiratory protection is always important.

2) T or F, in order to determine when a full face piece, self-contained breathing apparatus is needed you must first perform the assessment.

3) When should you wear a self-contained breathing apparatus (SCBA)?

4) How do you protect yourself from an **"IDLH"** atmosphere?

5) T or F, atmospheric testing should be performed in order to determine the presence of toxins and the level of oxygen in the work area.

6) T or F, the medical questionnaire should be completed before it is time to wear the respirator.

7) What is a dust mask?

8) What is meant by a N95 and a N100 respirator cartridge?

9) T or F, The higher the filter efficiency the less filter leakage.

10) T or F, Level A protection will require the responder to wear an air purifying respirator (APR).

11. SITE CONTROLS

After you have assessed the situation, it is important that you establish the site controls.

Site controls should be established as soon as possible.

Site controls may consist of the site maps, the sites drainage controls, the wind direction, building locations and more

The student will understand that site controls are needed in order to reduce and stop the spread of contamination. These controls are necessary in order to protect the workers and the public.

The exclusion (hot) zone, the contamination reduction (warm) zone and the support (cold) zone can be very helpful in tracking the personnel who have or who has not entered work area, along with controlling contamination.

These site controls can be used to help or to assist in the job going smoothly.

Site controls will consist of site preparation, work zones, establishing waste accumulation areas, the decontamination corridor and more.

Site controls are also need to **protect the site from vandalism**.

1) How do you establish the exclusion (hot) zone, the work area?

2) What is the purpose of a job briefing or a safety meeting?

3) T or F, when establishing the decontamination corridor, the wind direction is important.

4) T or F, a site map is not needed during site controls.

5) When should you establish site controls?

6) T or F, the purpose of site controls is to implement a procedure that is designed to protect the workers and the public.

7) T or F, any equipment entering the work zone must be decontaminated.

8) T or F, the decontamination procedures is a part of site controls.

9) What is meant by the contamination reduction zone?

10) What are the duties and the responsibilities of the personnel in the support zone?

12. HEALTH AND SAFETY PLAN

This section is designed to educate the student on the importance of developing and reviewing an accurate site health and safety plan.

The students will understand that a health and safety plan is a working document that should be modified as needed.

The HASP is a document that is designed to identify all of the site hazards.

This is the only document that you can use in order to track any and all of the efforts made to control or to mitigate the site hazards.

The HASP will identify all of the site safety hazards and it should also Include the sites emergency procedures.

The student/the reader will learn that the chemical and/or biological hazards are not the only hazards for the site.

The site hazards may range from the environment, to the above ground and the below ground electrical hazards, to slip, trips and even falls. All of these hazards should be identified in the plan.

It is recommended that every one that works on the site review, understand the site hazards and sign off on the health and safety plan.

1)   T or F the HASP is only needed when wearing level A protection.

2) Give an example of a person or the persons responsible for the completion of the health and safety plan.

3) T or F, the HASP shall be consistent with the other site plans.

4) T or F, if you work on a remediation site it is always necessary to complete a HASP.

5) T or F, The health and safety plan should only be review by the workers in the exclusion (hot) zone.

6) T or F, the health and safety plan can be used to describe and to select what type of personal protection equipment is needed.

7) T or F, the health and safety plan should have signatures of all of the workers and the site personnel who have reviewed the plan.

8) What is the purpose of a health and safety plan?

9) If you are visiting a hazardous waste site for the first time. What is the one way to become familiar with the site?

10) T or F, the site health and safety plan should include things like the location of the first-aid kits, along with the safety procedure and what should be done in the event of a injury or if there is a fire.

13. MONITORING/TESTING

The student will gain the ability to determine the differences between air monitoring and gas testing, along with the ability to identify or know when they are needed.

You can always provide gas testing and air monitoring. But you can only monitor or test for the concentrations of the known chemicals, biological agents or gases.

This can only be done after the assessment.....................................

You can test for the know gases, and then you monitor for the changes in the gases that you found during your testing?

Remember one method is used to detect the presence of the hazardous materials.

While the other method is designed to measure for quantities and concentrations of the hazardous materials detected.

The student will become familiar with the different tools, the different types of equipment and the latest technologies used for testing and monitoring.

The student must also be familiar with the units of measurement, be able to select the proper PPE, along with a monitoring program designed to protect all of the site personnel.

1)   Briefly describe the differences between **gas testing and air monitoring**.

2)   What is a four (4) gas meter?

3)   T or F, gas testing or air monitoring is a very effective tool when it comes to establishing site controls.

4)   T or F, there is one type of air monitoring or piece of gas testing equipment.

5)   What is meant by continuous monitoring?

6)   What does the expression "real time" refer too?

7)   Give an example of when it may be necessary to provide gas testing.

8) What are the four (4) gases we test for in the four gas meter?

9) What is the difference between continuous and periodic monitoring?

10) What is meant by (PPM) parts per million?

14. EMERGENCY RESPONSE

This is the portion of the manual where the students will learn to use the skills and the abilities previous learned in the training.

The student must have the ability to identify the chemical hazardous, have the basic skills of chemistry, the fundamental knowledge of toxicology, the ability to establish site controls, the ability to select PPE and the ability to establish the decontamination procedures, along with a waste management program.

Emergency response is when you are put to the test.

No two incidents are the same and every incident will pose its own unique hazards. The key is to look at the big picture and to break the incident down into sections.

The emergency response incident can be divided into **six (6) sections**; the event, the assessment, the identification of site hazards, the mitigation of the hazards, the creation of a plan and the conclusion.

The student must understand when developing a team that diversity and flexibility is important. Everyone on the team will have a role or responsibility to play and they must take that role or responsibility seriously

It is also important for us to see the need ***to open and to establish an effective line of communication*** with the various participating agencies.

1) What is the first thing you should do as an emergency responder after you have received the call?

2) T of F, as an emergency responder your job is to rush in and make the incident go away.

3) T or F, all hazardous materials will pose the same hazards.

4) How does the emergency response team establish the location for the command post?

5) T or F, the assessment of the incident should start immediately.

6) T or F, occasionally an emergency response event can be so extreme that it is sometimes best to let the incident take its course.

7) T or F, when it comes to building a team, diversity and flexibility are an important part of the team, especially when it comes to training.

8)   T or F, it is only necessary to identify the chemical hazards.

9)   What is difference between responding to an incident with a chemical release versus one with a biological agent?

10) What is the purpose of the **contamination reduction zone**?

15. EMERGENCY RESPONSE REHABILITAION

If the protection of the worker is the most important assets, then you must have a plan in place to **revitalize the worker** at the end of the shift or the end of the response.

Rehabilitation is definitely needed in emergency response because we will respond with a since of urgency, **work long hours with little rest**.

The student/the reader will understand that some events may last for a couple of hours, while others may **go on for days**.

The planned sites or the remediation projects will have to have something in place for the full time workers.

The rehabilitation station or stations can be something as simple as **a five (5) gallon** bucket under **a shade tree**, to something as elaborate as a **fully equipped mobile trailer with showers, air conditioned** with seating arrangements.

It is important to keep the **worker well-nourished and hydrated**.

The decontamination station and the rehabilitation station should be **set up before they are needed.**

1)   T or F, heat stress and dehydration can be a major problem for the worker or the emergency responder.

2) Where should the rehabilitation station be set up?

3) T or F, it is alright to go through rehabilitation before decontamination.

4) T or F, the support zone and the cold zones are one in the same.

5) What is meant by the term **"position of comfort"**?

6) T or F, The rehabilitation station is only designed for the workers in the exclusion zone, explain.

7) What is the **purpose of the backup team**?

8) Who is responsible for establishing the workers rehabilitation station?

9) T or F, the workers should be evaluated for chemical, for biological exposure and for changes in their vital signs during rehabilitation.

10) T or F, the emergency medical personnel can play a key role in the workers rehabilitation process.

16. DECOTAMINATION

The students must understand the importance of sending the workers home the same way they came.

The student will learn that the decontamination procedures should be put in place immediately.

After you have identified the chemical/the biological hazards' a plan should put in place to mitigate or to remove those hazards.

The decontamination plan should be a part of the health and safety plan.

Decontamination procedure **should focus** on the **removal of contaminates.**

This can be as simple as water hose, a five gallon bucket, with kiddy pool or as elaborate as a large decontamination trailer fully equipped with showers and dressing rooms.

The student/the reader will learn the **two (2) types** of **decontamination** and based on your assessment you will determine which type of decontamination is best.

Any equipment or personal protection equipment, along with the solutions used for decontamination must be properly disposed of.

1) What are the **two (2) types** of decontamination?

2) What is the purpose of decontamination?

3) T or F, decontamination must consist of a sequence of operation designed to remove the contamination and the disposal of the PPE.

4) T or F, decontamination procedures should be set up before the team makes its entry.

5) Give an example of how the team would provide decontamination for a **class 4.3** hazardous material.

6) What is meant by emergency decontamination?

7) T or F, one of the keys to an effective decontamination program is to have in place **"Standard Operating Procedures".**

8) T or F, before you can establish the contamination reduction zone (**the decontamination corridor**) you must first establish the exclusion (hot) zone.

9) Where do you stage the waste material that has been accumulated in the decontamination process?

10) T or F in order to control the spread of contamination there shall only be one entry point and only one exit point into the work area.

17. INCIDENT COMMAND

When it comes to emergency response, especially chemical spill response, this industry is divided into two sections; the private sector and the public sector.

The **public sector** focuses on the safety and the protection of the public.

The **private sector** is charged with the responsibility of handling any emergencies or incidents, which they may be responsible for.

The health and safety plan should focus on the protection of the workers, the environment and the protection of the public.

Each sector has its own priorities and responsibilities.

The public sector may use the **IC System daily** while the private sector will only use ICS if or as it is needed. Basically the incident or events will have to be large enough that it affects the public.

The incident command system adds additional structure to the incidents; it opens an effective line of communication between the various participating agencies. The IC System will allow the team to focus on the work.

The incident commander is located in the command post and he or she is responsible for implementing a communications system for the various agencies and the team.

The incident commander must have the **working knowledge of the incident** that he or she is in charge of, especially if they expect to be successful.

The incident command system can be a very effective and useful tool.

1) What is the purpose of the incident command system?

2) T or F, the fire services (public safety) have been using the incident command system for years.

3) T or F, because you work in public safety means you have been trained in hazardous materials chemical spill response.

4) What role does public safety play if you are employed as emergency responders?

5) What role does the logistics officer play?

6) Give an example of and explain what is meant by public safety?

7) T or F, the IC system is designed to open up an effective line of communication between the various participating agencies.

8) How would you structure the command post if you had to respond to a grade crossing collision accident multiple injuries and a bulk hazardous material release?

18. REMEDIATION

The student/the reader must be able to understand the differences between remediation and the emergency response.

Basically with **remediation** you will **have the time** and luxury **to schedule** the work. You are not in a hurry therefore you have the time to do your duties safely.

During remediation you will need to establish a health and safety plan, establish site controls, the selection of personnel protection equipment, decontamination procedures, and even the waste disposal options.

Remember remediation activities can range from something as simple as the decontamination of a building, to the removal of contaminated soils, to the excavation of an underground storage tanks (UST), to the disposal of abandon drums.

You must remember that the **worker's safety** must **never** be **compromised**.

Even though you have an established a schedule, a game plan, you should *never be in hurry to get someone injured or exposed*.

1) What is the one thing that you should remember about remediation, when it comes to the cleanup efforts?

2) T or F, you must establish site controls for remediation projects.

3) T or F, decontamination is necessary during remediation.

4) Just like in emergency response, what is the one thing you should always do before you start your remediation efforts?

5) T or F, establishing a work schedule or opening an effective line of communication is not important during remediation.

6) T or F, a job briefing and/or a safety meeting is not a part of the site activity or necessary during the remediation event?

7) T or F, one of the ways to establish remediation is to bring emergency responses incident under control.

8) Give me an example how you would prepare a site that last contained a class six (6) hazardous materials leaking from a 55 gallon drum.

9) T or F, one of the benefits to remediation is you have the time to plan and the time to establish a schedule.

19. TREATMENT, STORAGE AND DISPOSAL

When there is **no further use for the material**. The materials will have to be disposed of and **any material classified as a hazardous waste is regulated** by the federal government.

All hazardous waste will have to be properly managed by the generator or potential responsible party (PRP).

Remember a hazardous waste can either be **characteristic or listed**

A **characteristic waste** can be ignitable, corrosive, reactive and/or toxic

Once you have determined that the material is a hazardous waste, you must also determine the source of generation.

A **listed waste** can come from a specific source, a non-specific source, it can be a raw material or it can be an acutely hazardous raw material.

Remember when you are accumulating waste and establishing the waste codes it is important that you know where and how the waste was generated.

There are several options when it comes to handling waste. These options may consist of incineration, another is solidification, and then you have fuels blending, flaring for flammables, neutralization for the corrosives and even land filling.

The large quantity generator must have a hazardous waste accumulation area, a container packaging and labeling policy, along with that they must comply with the waste accumulation, storage and handling requirements.

The generator must have a contingency plan and the hazardous waste must be segregated, properly containerized, with the appropriate labels and markings.

All hazardous waste when transported must be accompanied by an ***unformed hazardous waste manifest and waste profile sheets.***

1)   What is the definition of a hazardous waste?

2)   T or F, a hazardous waste management program should be one of the first things you establish during an incident with a release.

3)   Give an example of a least two techniques that can be used to dispose of a flammable liquid.

4)   T or F, all hazardous waste are given and identified by hazardous waste codes.

5)   A hazardous waste that can be disposed of by neutralization is considered what type of waste?

6) What is a Disposal option for a hazardous material that is a corrosive?

7) T or F, the generator is responsible for the hazardous waste material from "cradle to grave"?

8) Which hazardous waste codes are assigned to an acutely toxic material?9) What is difference between a generator and potential responsible party?10) T or F, the large quantity generator must provide weekly inspections of the hazardous waste accumulation area.

9) What is the difference between the generator and the potential responsible party?

10) T or F, the large quantity generator must provide weekly inspections of the hazardous waste accumulation areas.

20. CONFINED SPACE ENTRY

In order to determine if the work area has confined spaces you must perform an accurate assessment.

The confined spaces must be identified and placed in the health and safety plan.

There are two (2) types of confined spaces that can be identified; **a permit required space** and a **non-permit required space**.

In order for these areas to be classified as a confined space they must met three (3) criteria.

The manpower will also consist of three (3) types of individuals.

The person's participating in the confined space entry activities will either be a supervisor, an attendant or an entrants.

After you have identified all of the confined spaces on the site and you have made an effort to control the hazards or to get rid of those of the hazards. You can establish a permit as needed.

You should only enter the work area (the confined space) after you have made every effort **to mitigate the hazards** and you have **generated a permit** as needed.

1) What is the definition of a confined space?

2) T or F, a permit required confided space can either be an above ground storage tank or an underground storage tank.

3) Who is responsible for the completion of the confined space entry permit?

4) What role does the attendant play?

5) What are the four gases you will test for with the four (4) gas meter?

6) What is the definition of engineering controls?

7) What should be done if you are currently operating under a permit and there is an atmospheric change?

8) T or F, one of the first things you should do is make sure that you have breathable air.

9)   If you are currently working under a permit, what must be done if the entrant has to exit the work area?

10) T or F, toxic gases can either be **heavier or lighter than air.**

21. SITE SAFETY

The employers have taken the safety of their workers (personnel) serious; therefore they have to incorporate a system that is designed to protect the workers.

The employer understands if you are an emergency responder you will be required to seek some additional safety training which can and will be useful with your response efforts.

Each incident is **different** and will pose its **own unique hazards**; therefore you must have the ability to be **flexible** and the ability to **see the big picture**.

All hazardous waste sites may post some of the same unique hazards but the biggest problem in this day and age is the distractions.

These distractions may come in a variety of different ways; one of the biggest distractions is electronic devices.

These devices may have a variety of different uses on the hazardous waste site and they are everywhere, but they can pose their own unique hazards.

1) T or F, before a person can start work on a hazardous waste site they should review the **site's health and safety plan**.

2) T or F, all site hazards are the same, explain.

3) T or F, electronic devices can be a major safety hazards if used incorrectly in the work area.

4) Give an example of some additional site safety hazards.

5) Give an example of some **additional safety training** you should take if you wish to become **successful** as a hazardous materials technician supervisor.

6) The hazardous materials technician/emergency responder that is trained at the awareness level has the ability too?

7) T or F, lock-out/tag-out can play a key role in confined space entry especially if there is an electrical source involved.

8) What is meant by a job briefing?

9) T or F, after you have completed your initial forty (40) hours of training you will have the ability to perform high pressure gas transfers.

10) Which federal regulations focus on the safety of the workers?

22. CONCLUSION

This is not the end of your training, but only the beginning, especially if you are participating in emergency response.

I recommend that you go out and learn as much as you can, if you are planning on being around for any extended period of time, you must recognize that the site hazards and conditions are real.

Remember as you go forward with your career especially in emergency response that there are always continuing updates and upgrades.

You can always find the latest, the greatest and the newest equipment. Just don't compromise your safety.

A toxic material is a toxic material, a flammable material is flammable material, a corrosive is a corrosive and an infectious substance (biological agent) is an infectious substance, if you always treat these materials as the worst case scenario you will never go wrong.

Remember this workbook is not designed to replace the student trianing manual, but is designed to enhance the material that should have been covered and received during your initial training.

This workbook/exam is dedicated to;

The men and women that have dedicated their lives, to helping others, the men and women that have and will stand the test of time, to the men and women who realize that every incident will have its own unique hazards, to the men and women that see the importance of going home safely, to the men and women that have the ability to stay focused.

A special thanks to Dave G. and Nick A. with Ecovac Services for standing the test of time in enhanced fluid recovery and allowing me to provide the personnel with over twenty plus years of continuing education and training.